BLOODY KINGS AND KILLER QUEENS OF London

First published in 2003 by Watling St Publishing
The Glen
Southrop
Lechlade
Gloucestershire
GL7 3NY

Printed in Italy

ISBN 1-904153-16-X

24681097531

Design: Maya Currell
Cover design and illustration: Mark Davis
Cartoons: Martin Angel

Bloody Kings and Killer Queens of London

Natasha Narayan

WATLING STREET

Natasha Narayan has worked as a journalist in Albania, Bosnia, Georgia and the former Soviet Union. She was also briefly education correspondent on the *Observer*, a waitress, and a satellite TV presenter. She lives in North London with her husband, daughter and son.

This book is dedicated to Paul with love.

Contents

INTRODUCTION

This book is about London's bloodiest kings and queens. They're not a particularly nice mob. You might not want to meet any of them down a dark alley – and you certainly wouldn't want to get in their black books.

I've had to pick and choose. I've left out some B grade nasties, those mildly murderous kings and queens who pale in comparison next to some of the foul, loathsome and spectacularly vile kings and queens who have graced these shores. The sort who wouldn't think twice about murdering an inconvenient relative or two before tea.

But apart from frequently being quite literally bloody awful to their friends, family, and most of all, their long-suffering subjects - many of these monarchs had a pretty rough time themselves.

Elizabeth I saw her own mother Anne Boleyn executed at her father's behest. If you know any friendly shrinks ask them how that rates in terms of childhood trauma?

And poor James I. He saw practically his whole family and a series of guardians foully murdered before he got his sticky fingers on the English crown.

As time went on kings and queens got a little less bloody. This isn't because they got nicer but because they had less power. In the old days if a king or queen took a dislike to someone they could pretty much order 'off with their heads'. More modern monarchs have had to cope, poor things, with inconvenient things like Parliament and laws, which put a stop to their more outrageous behaviour. So much so that our current queen, Elizabeth II, seems like a pussycat, compared with her namesake, Elizabeth I.

CHAPTER ONE

Bill the Bruiser

In 1066, as England's dreamy king, Edward the Confessor*
was newly laid in his grave, a blazing comet with a fiery red
tail was seen in the spring skies. Many people thought it was
an omen of terrible times to come. Boy, were they right.
Later that year one of the bloodiest of our bloody kings
was crowned in London's Westminster Abbey.

(*He wasn't called this because he had an addiction to
owning up to bad things he'd done but because of his
saintly status.)

Now, Edward had upset some of his Saxon compatriots by
getting a bit too friendly with the Normans across the
Channel. So friendly in fact that the Duke of Normandy,
better known to us as William the Conqueror, thought that
the Crown should pass to him. And to add insult to injury,
William was illegitimate, not a great thing to be in those
days if you wanted to be king. (His nickname The Bastard
referred to his birth, not his character, though you might
be forgiven for thinking otherwise ...)

William took charge of England, after invading the island
with a posse of Normans and killing its newly crowned king,

Harold Godwinson, in the bloody Battle of Hastings. William insisted that Harold had promised him England when he'd helped him out of a tight spot a few years before. Harold said he hadn't. Whatever the truth, William was able to convince the pope (who was very, very important and powerful) that Harold was a liar and got lots of French nobles to throw in their men and money on the promise of the juicy spoils of victory.

And William was the first king to be a true Londoner. He was the first monarch to set up his main court in London – in Westminster.

PLACE: Westminster Abbey

DATE: Christmas Day 1066

EVENT: The Coronation of William the Conqueror.

The vast church is filled with the highest in the land – nobles and ladies, bishops and priests. Towering above all of them is the imposing figure of the Conqueror, all five feet ten of him (quite tall in those days). His red hair glittering in the candlelight, William advances towards the altar where the two churchmen – one Norman, Geoffrey Bishop of Coustance, and one English, Aedelred of York, are waiting to crown him king.

Inside the church is filled with incense and perfume. Outside the street is packed with the smelly mass of wary and hostile Londoners. William's fierce knights stand guard, under orders to arrest anyone who is not happy enough!

WILLIAM: (Walking up to altar) Alright, Bish, get on with it. Haven't got all day. Got wars to fight.

The bishops proceed with the solemn rites of the coronation of King William I. The oaths are taken and then King William is about to be anointed with sacred oil.

THE CONGREGATION: (Under orders to be loudly joyful) VIVAT KING WILLIAM, VIVAT KING WILLIAM.

As the guards hear the shouting from within the Abbey they conclude that an attack is taking place and do what they always do – set fire to every building in sight. Smoke pours into the Abbey and the terrified nobles rush out. Soon the whole of Westminster is burning.

BISHOP: *(Alarmed)* For Godsake's, what's happening? *(To William)* 'Scuse my French, won't you? Lost my head with all the panic.

WILLIAM: You'll lose your head for real, you silly oaf, if you don't get on with it.

Only the priests remain in Westminster to complete the big ceremony. The rest of the congregation have rushed outside in blind terror. As the bishop completes the coronation, the nobles are fighting the flames, or hoping to take the opportunity for a spot of looting.

William's big day as the new king of England was a farce. No wonder that he concluded the English couldn't be trusted and set about building the Tower of London. He needed somewhere to keep his jewels, wife and person safe – and, equally important, a place to keep the English yobs out.

The first tower to go up, near the famous London Bridge, was made of wood. A few years later another thick limestone tower, which is now the basis of the central White Tower, was designed by a monk called Gandulf.

William was now king of England and decided to pop back to Normandy for a bit of rest and relaxation – and also a spot more war. But while he was away revolts broke out all over the country.

12

Now William really showed his true colours. From 1069 to 1070 his soldiers cut a swathe through the land, burning, pillaging, raping and brutally putting to death anyone who got in his way. In large patches of the north, all the crops were burned down – so those who weren't killed by Will's soldiers died slowly from hunger and starvation.

One writer described infected corpses decaying in the streets. Survivors ate cats and dogs and sold themselves as slaves. No village was left inhabited between Durham and York and the land was left unploughed for eight years.

The entire English landed class of barons – who had led the revolt - were wiped out. Their land was given to Will's Norman friends, who became the new rulers. The fact they didn't even speak the native lingo didn't endear the new bosses to their subjects – those who were left alive.

'Foreigners,' wrote the half-Norman monk Orderic Vitalis, 'grew wealthy with the spoils of England while her own sons were either shamefully slain or driven as exiles to wander hopelessly.'

Will, by this time, wasn't too keen on England. He even gave up trying to learn English. Apart from a useful source of loot, he saw it as a sort of holiday camp and turned miles of it over to his favourite sport, hunting. Villagers were

kicked out of their homes to
create the huge New Forest
in Hampshire. Poachers, even
those who gathered sticks on
royal land, were blinded and
mutilated.

But one class of men have
occasion to remember William fondly – tax collectors. In
1086 he devised the first great system for squeezing more
tax out of people, the *Domesday Book*.

His minions went to every hamlet and pile of mud and
wattle in the land and jotted down what the inhabitants
owned – down to the last pig, sheep and cow pat. This was
put into a big book. All in the interests of more dosh for
Will and his wars!

The *Domesday Book* paints a picture of a miserably poor
England that toiled hard on the land. Half the good land in
England was in the hands of 170 barons, only two of whom
were English. The king personally owned a fifth of the land
and most of the rest was owned by the Church. London was
mostly left out of the book, though Stepenhede (Stepney)
and Chenesitun (Kensington) were put in as places where
cattle grazed. It's probable that William knew how wealthy
London was and didn't need to count every chicken.

WILLIAM'S CUT OUT AND KEEP
GUIDE TO FEUDALISM

One of William's greatest contributions to England was feudalism. Guess who was the biggest winner under feudalism? Yep, that's right, William.

1. THE KING: Owns all the land. Fat bloodsucker at top of pile.

2. BARONS, EARLS: Tenants in chief of huge bits of land but have to swear loyalty to the king. Also provide him with Knights and dosh for wars.

3. KNIGHTS: Rent land from the barons.

4. FREEMEN: Freehold tenants who pay tithe (rent or work on the land) to the Knights. They are free to leave the land.

5. SERFS, VILLEINS: Get miserable smallholding to farm. Have to give rent and work the Knights' fields. If they attempt to run away, they can be brought back to slave away.

In later life Will became so fat that one rival king said he looked like a pregnant woman. But his size didn't put him off his favourite sport – war. In July 1087 he died on his horse during a battle in France.

When the burial men tried to force his body into the stone coffin it burst and filled the church in Caen, France, with foul odours that sent the grieving congregation hurrying for their hankies.

Just a pleasant reminder of Will's sunny personality!

CORPSE COUNT: Some historians estimate that at least 300,000 people, one in five of the English population, were killed by William's soldiers or starved to death as they burnt their crops. The Normans soon made up for it, however, as in the twenty years after the invasion some 200,000 Normans settled in England.

TORTURE TALLY: William brought a special kind of cruelty to being king. He sanctioned the first beheading in England. One prisoner had his limbs slowly crushed on the king's personal orders.

CHAPTER TWO

Softsword John

King John ruled England from 1199 to 1216. He succeeded his brother Richard who was always popping off to fight in the Crusades. Richard was a dreamboat, tall with red-gold hair and blue eyes. He was nicknamed 'Lionheart'. John was short, not much to look at and was nicknamed 'Softsword', which doesn't have quite the same ring about it, does it? His other nickname was John Lackland because he, well, lacked land. As you can imagine, people didn't think he was a patch on his big bro.

But he did have his good points. Well, sort of.

NICE THINGS ABOUT KING JOHN

1. He liked hot baths. The Middle Ages was a time when most people never bathed at all. (Even the handsome Lionheart.) King John would smell nicer (or at least less foul) than almost anyone else you would meet in London circa 1210.

2. He was very inventive. He is thought to have dreamed up the wheeze of pouring boiling pig fat down a long tunnel to crush resistance in a besieged castle. John used this clever idea in Rochester, Kent, to bring some rebels to heel.

SOME NOT SO VERY NICE THINGS ABOUT JOHNNY.

1. He tried to steal the Crown from his brother Richard, who was a bit careless with it, always going off to the Crusades. When Richard was captured in Austria John lost no time proclaiming himself king and seizing the Crown. Unfortunately for him, Richard was still alive. His ransom cost 34 tonnes of gold – three times the annual income of England.

2. He gave his mum, Eleanor of Aquitaine, grey hairs. She wrote in a letter to the Pope, 'I am an unhappy mother, pitied by no one ... two sons remain but they exist to add to my miseries. King Richard is in irons; his brother John ravages the kingdom with fire and sword.'

3. He murdered his nephew. Arthur, Duke of Brittany, was the son of his older brother Geoffrey and the rightful heir to the throne. John took twelve-year-old Arthur prisoner in a dawn raid on a castle in Normandy, where he was hiding out with his grandmother Eleanor. Apparently King John was cheesed off when the cocky Arthur refused to acknowledge

him as king. So one evening when he had had too much booze at dinner, he stuck his sword through him. (Not so 'softsword' then). He tied a heavy stone to Arthur's body and threw it in the River Seine.

4. He stole another man's fiancée, the pretty heiress Isabella of Angoulême.

5. He hanged one of his wife's admirers from one of her bedposts.

John had the ability to get right up people's noses. The furious fiancé of Isabella – a nobleman named Hugh of Lusignan – got the king of France's help in cobbling together an army against John. He was pretty much driven out of Normandy, which his family had owned for yonks.

John now escaped to England and spent the next eight years taxing the hell out of his subjects to raise money for his war against the French. In 1215 the English barons, along with some important citizens of London, captured the city, presenting John with a list of demands – the Barons' Charter or Magna Carta.

The Magna Carta had nothing to say about the rights of villeins and serfs – but it did have plenty to say about how the king couldn't take the mickey out of the landowners.

One right said that no freeman could be arrested without the lawful judgement of his peers, the origin of the jury.

But John really didn't like this newfangled charter. He used to go back to his castle every evening and roll on the floor in a rage. Blue spots appeared on his face during his fits and he would start eating the straw that covered the floor. He was quite a weird bloke, really.

But John was forced to sign the Magna Carta at Runnymede, an island on the Thames near Windsor. But no sooner did he sign it than he took it all back. He claimed he was tricked. The bolshy barons got the King of France to help them. A French army landed in Kent and marched towards London.

John now got his own army together and retreated across away from London, burning crops and pillaging as he went.

But luck was not on his side. Or perhaps he was too impatient. Crossing the Neck of the Wash, in East Anglia, the tide came in. John watched as his mules, laden with sacks of gold and jewels, sank slowly out of sight.

The loss of his loot upset John more than the loss of those lives. Utterly miserable, he comforted himself like he always did. With a good feed.

It was one pig-out too far. After too many peaches and pints of sweet ale he contracted dysentery and died. John had literally guzzled himself to death.

CHAPTER THREE

Dick Dastardly

There are two versions of the King Richard III story floating around:

1) Ruthless Richard

He was a wicked villain with a withered arm, a humpback and a cold, twisted heart. When his brother King Edward IV was dying in 1483 Richard promised to protect his two young sons. The elder son, also called Edward, who was just twelve years old, was supposed to become king once he was a man. Instead Richard had his angelic nephews cruelly murdered in the Tower of London and then stole the Crown for himself. Everything he did was motivated by an insane lust for power. Thank God brave Henry Tudor (King Henry VII) killed him in the Battle of Bosworth in 1485!

2) Misunderstood Richard

He was a brave, intelligent man and a fine ruler who wanted to clean up England after his brother's corrupt reign. If he had a fault, he was a bit too hasty. He alienated many nobles in his Keep England Clean campaign. After he was defeated by villainous Henry VII, the Tudor lot decided to rewrite history to justify the new king's seizure of the crown. (This is called propaganda – and you should never believe everything you read. Except this, of course.)

Tame hacks in the pay of the Tudors, like some young playwright bloke called William Shakespeare, let's say exaggerated the truth a bit. They blamed Richard for lots of crimes he didn't commit, like the murder of his wife and the murder of his brother the Duke of Clarence. They even invented the story of his hunchback and withered arm. In those days, most people thought that any kind of disability meant you were bad or being punished for something. Nice!

So which story is true? Was Dastardly Dick the most repulsive ruler ever to bestride the throne? Was he the bloody king to end all bloody kings? Or was he a decent sort of bloke who was unlucky enough to get in the way of the Tudor Twisters?

The problem with giving you a definite answer is that all this happened a long, long time ago. There aren't many accounts of King Richard's brief two-and-a-half-year reign that were written at the time. We can't examine the corpses detective-style with our microscopes. We can't hand down a guilty or innocent verdict in a court of law.

But we can try and figure out what seems likely to be true.

Spot the Difference

Here are two descriptions of
Richard. Which one do you
think was written at the time
and which was a later Tudor
view?

A) 'Richard was three feet taller than (myself), but a little
slimmer, less thick set and much more lean as well; he had
delicate arms and legs also a great heart.'

B) 'Malicious, wrathful envious', 'little of stature, ill
featured of limbs, crook backed, his left shoulder much
higher than his right', 'lowly of countenance, arrogant of
heart, outwardly companionable where inwardly he hated'.

ANSWER:

A) was written by German diplomat Nicholas Von Poppelau,
who stayed in one of Richard's castles with him, in 1485.
This was before Richard was killed. Altogether six accounts
of Richard from the time he lived don't mention his
supposedly glaring deformities and humps!

B) is from Sir Thomas More's description of Richard in his
unfinished *History of Richard III* written around 1513.

It seems likely that Richard did have a slightly higher shoulder on one side. (There is no smoke without a fire and, besides, anyone writing at the time might have been a bit nervous about mentioning any irregular features.) This was later turned by Tudor re-write artists into the hump-backed ogre of Shakespeare's creation. Here's how Richard describes himself at the beginning of Shakespeare's play, *Richard III*

> **Deform'd, unfinish'd, sent before my time**
> **Into this breathing world, scarce half made up,**
> **And that so lamely and unfashionable**
> **That dogs bark at me as I halt by them**

Most of the mythmaking came from Sir Thomas More's account. But Richard's opponents point out that Sir Thomas had good sources who lived at the time - including his own dad, who had been a pal of Richard's and other important clerics.

Other Tudors went even further. A priest called John Rous, writing in about 1491, claimed Richard came out into the world after a stunning two years in his mother's womb (the average period is nine months). Apparently this demon baby Richard had teeth, hair down to his shoulders, a hump back and his right shoulder higher than his left!

The Tudor monsterization of Richard wasn't just verbal. They got to work repainting his pictures too. If you go to the National Portrait Gallery in Central London you can see a painting of Richard III. X-rays taken in the past fifty years show that the right shoulder has been painted over on the original to make it look deformed. And the eyes have been narrowed to make them look slitty and mean!

But the Tudors didn't just claim that Richard was no victor in the good looks stakes. They said he was the bloodiest of bloody kings. He was so vicious, they claim, he was even responsible for a series of cruel murders right on his own doorstep.

1) King Killer?

King Henry VI (1437-1461 and 1470-71) was an unusual sort of king for those nasty times. He was saintly, suffered from epilepsy and was much more interested in god than in the crown. And there were plenty of people ready to wrest the crown from him, chief among them Edward Plantagenet (Richard's brother), who became Edward IV.

When Edward assumed the Crown for the second time in 1471, after a lot of battles, poor old saintly Henry was locked in the Tower. (There aren't many English kings who you can use the word saintly about. Bloody, well that's another matter!) Then he was mysteriously murdered.

Ed's new government pretended that Henry was so cheesed off with being locked up that he died of 'displeasure'. But he was spotted bleeding to death on the road.

So who killed this holy royal simpleton? Lots of the Tudor writers say Richard did. Some say he stuck King Henry VI through with his own dagger.

But it seems very unlikely that Richard could have killed a king without his brother's consent. The new king, his brother, was the one who really benefited from poor Henry's death.

2) Brother killer?

Richard's brother the Duke of Clarence was a real trouble-maker. He led an armed rebellion against his other brother, King Edward IV, mainly because he wanted to get his greasy behind on the throne. After he stormed into a state meeting and accused the king of being a bastard and his wife of sorcery Edward got sick of him and locked him up in the Tower. He was tried for treason and sentenced to be executed. In February 1478 Clarence died at the Tower, probably by drowning in a butt of malmsey wine. There is no real evidence to saddle Richard with the murder. In fact one writer of the time said he was 'overcome with grief'.

3) Wife killer?

Richard's wife Anne Neville died in March 1485. Richard wept openly by her grave. But rumours were already sweeping London, reported as fact by later Tudor propagandists, that he poisoned

her. The gossips said he wanted to marry his own niece, dead King Ed's daughter Elizabeth of York.

Young Elizabeth was said to be infatuated with her old uncle and also - more to the point - keen to be queen.

But after his wife's death the scandal of Richard's interest in his niece was too damaging for it to continue. Richard denied he ever wanted to marry her. Elizabeth was sent away from London because Richard was scared that his mortal enemy Henry Tudor had his eye on her - and the wealth and title to the crown that she would bring. In fact Elizabeth did end up marrying Henry Tudor.

The claim that Richard poisoned his wife has never been proved. Some think Anne may have died of a broken heart. She and Richard were grief-stricken when their only son died.

4) Nephew killer?

This is the Big Bad Crime. The cold-blooded murder of two innocent, defenceless children whom Richard had sworn to protect is a very monstrous murder indeed. Even in an age of monster murders it stood out.

It is the nasty crime that has forever had Richard down in history's bad books. But did he do it?

❋ ❋ ❋

THE TOWER OF LONDON VISITORS BOOK

Prince Edward Plantaganet

2 September 1483

I am scared of tomorrow. I am twelve years old but already haunted by bad dreams. What can I tell my younger brother? Poor little Richard is only ten, still a child. I am forced to be a man though not allowed to be king.

My uncle Richard visits us here – in this damp dungeon – only in my nightmares. Yet a few months ago he was so good to me. There was never a kinder or more loving uncle. He played games with us. I thought my father had chosen a good man to look after us. But then Richard turned traitor. He declared me and my brother were bastards and stole my crown!

He lied. Vile lies. I am as royal as anyone. My mum would never have allowed me to be a bastard. So there.

Now, on my uncle's orders, we are caged like rats in this dark place. We can't even stand at the window. I am sick. My bones ache. My flesh aches. I am wasting away. It is just not fair. I don't know if my mother and sisters are dead or alive. My attendants, my tutors, my friends have gone all gone. Now I have only these horrid brutes around me. Five beastly gaolers to guard me and my small brother.

Where are my soft clothes and my lovely horse? And my new riding boots? Why do we only have rough bread and water to eat?

No one, I think, cares what happens to us. We are truly forgotten.

I dread that Richard plans to murder us. I would willingly give up the crown and leave this whole nasty country if he would spare our lives. I've never done anything to hurt him!

3 September 1483 was the most likely date picked for the evil deed.

At the stroke of midnight dark figures stole in while the two little golden-haired boys slept in their feather beds. The killers placed a pillow over each boy's face. Struggling, kicking, crying out, the princes were quickly suffocated to death.

Their bodies were taken and buried under a lump of stones at the foot of the Tower.

But who ordered the killing?

Richard was sitting on the loo whingeing on and on to his page. Nobody would obey him and kill the nuisance princes, he whined. The murder was just too vile. Then the page had a brilliant idea. Why don't you try Sir James Tyrell? he suggested. Tyrell was an ambitious nobleman who slept outside Richard's door as a kind of guard. He would do anything to get on in the world, the page said.

Tyrell was chosen. He shrank from the killing himself. So he picked a few goons, including one of the princes' own guards, to carry out the murder.

This is the story told by Thomas More, who got his information from Tyrell's confession. (A confession that mysteriously disappeared.) But what hard evidence do we have that the princes really were murdered in the Tower?

In 1674, almost two centuries after their disappearance, the skeletons of two little boys were found buried beneath a staircase in the White Tower at the Tower of London. From their ages and where they were found it was immediately assumed that they were the little princes. In 1933 the skeletons were medically tested and from their bone structure it was proved that they were aged about ten and twelve, the ages of the little princes when they died in the autumn of 1483.

But there are some historian-detectives who still claim Richard didn't order the princes' murder. But if it wasn't Richard, who murdered the princes?

Pick a Killer

1. Henry Tudor, the man who became King Henry VII.

A) Strangely a whole year after he defeated Richard at the Battle of Bosworth Henry issued two royal pardons to James Tyrell, who went on to become his faithful servant for sixteen years.

B) He never directly blamed Richard for the murders. Why

not, when it was a propaganda gift from heaven?

C) Two years after he became king he was suddenly very nasty to his mum-in-law, who was the princes' mum, and had her locked up. Was it because she had learnt that the scheming Tudor king ordered the murder of her sons?

But pinning the blame on Henry Tudor just doesn't stand up because of the ages of the two boy skeletons found buried in the Tower. Henry would not have been able to kill the princes when they were ten and twelve – he was in exile in Europe.

2. The Duke of Buckingham

He was very a powerful noble who led an armed rebellion against Richard. Basically Buckingham wanted the throne too – and the little princes were in the way. But again the story doesn't stand up. It is very unlikely Buckingham could have got into the Tower without Richard's permission. Plus if Buckingham was guilty why didn't Richard say so – instead of shouldering the blame for the rest of history?

3. No one

Killing children is an act too awful to think of. Even in the murderous Middle Ages. Some ingenious historians have suggested that the princes were smuggled to secret hiding places (in the country, or abroad) and given new identities. But there is silence about this, everywhere. Surely someone would have known. And then there are those two inconvenient skeletons. This theory is wishful thinking.

4. Richard

This leaves the favourite squarely in the frame. Let's face it, the other candidates for murder look distinctly dodgy. The young princes vanished and Richard III was crowned king. No one else reaped the rewards of their murder like their loving uncle did.

In the end you decide. Richard the monster? Or Richard the innocent victim of negative Tudor hype? Or Richard the fairly nasty? (My money is on Richard the nephew killer.)

Richard didn't have long to enjoy the fruits of his hideous crimes. As we know he was defeated by Henry Tudor at the Battle of Bosworth. Richard had few friends left. A large part of his army, under a big-shot noble, turned against him and joined his Tudor enemy.

Did Richard's conscience speak to him on the eve of his death? Several writers tell how the night before battle he suffered a terrible dream in which frightful demons crowded around him on all sides.

CORPSE COUNT: Killing people was all in a day's work for Richard as he grew up. Some, like Lord Hastings, whom he executed because he supported the young princes, are definite Richard victims. Some might add his wife and his nephews – though not his brother or his king. Still, a pretty bloody record.

TORTURE TALLY: Torture wasn't really Richard's style. He was nothing if not direct. He preferred to kill his victims straight out. Still, he gets torture points for locking up so many enemies in the Tower's dungeons.

PS Propaganda doesn't always go the way you want it to. If the Tudor Twisters hadn't used up so much ink trying to convince people that Richard was the nastiest villain ever we would probably have forgotten all about him by now. After all, he only ruled for a couple of years.

CHAPTER FOUR

Horrible Henry

When Henry VIII climbed onto the throne in 1508 his new subjects didn't guess he was horrible. They drooled, they swooned, they fell at his feet in droves. They thought he was IT. The last word in Princely Princes and Heavenly Heroes.

For a start, while most Tudors were pretty puny, handsome Harry was six foot two. He towered over other men. Ooh his hair was so glossy, ooh he was so muscly and hunky, ooh the diamonds sparkled and glittered on his fingers and throat. His skin seemed to glow through his shirt, one lovestruck courtier gasped as he watched Henry play tennis.

'He is the handsomest monarch I have ever set eyes upon,' gushed the Venetian ambassador in 1515, 'with a round face so very beautiful it would become a pretty woman.'

In fact Henry was more like a pop idol than a boring old

monarch. He was the first English king to have his own band, which followed him round strumming away at their lutes. (As you might guess Henry was lead vocals!) The wenches used to go gaga when Henry and his band came to town. He was so glamourous all the men wanted to be him.

Here is a rap Henry might have sung about himself. (Modesty was never one of his traits!):

Henry the handsome, Henry the hip
Six feet two from toe to tip
A whiz at jousting and on the horse
I can beat all at battle and on the course

Damsels flock wherever I wander
They pray to me to take them yonder
Knights are mine in heart and soul
For I am the king who owns them whole
(chorus)
A king to flog them, a king so grand
A king to rule, a king for fair England
A king, a hero, a god, a superstar
A king to worship from near and far

But twenty-five years later the tune had changed. Henry still thought himself impossibly glamourous. In fact he was so fat he would have been given up as a dead loss by Weightwatchers. He no longer shone in jousting, riding and tennis. He walked or rather waddled with difficulty. In one of his palaces they built a special, supersize handcart to wheel him from room to room. All of his castles had to have a complicated system of ropes and pulleys to hoist him up the stairs.

In his later years Henry wasn't the sweetest of companions. He suffered from foul moods, paranoia, sore legs, constipation and gout.

None of his nobles felt safe because it was said Henry had 'never made a man but he destroys them again' - i.e. you'd be in his good books on Tuesday and out again on Wednesday. Abroad people thought that Henry presided over a terrified people in a police state. 'In England,' they said, 'death has snatched up anyone of worth or fear has shrunk them up.'

The story of how Prince Charming turned into Horrible Henry is the story of how power turned a man's head. Right from the start Henry dominated his court, his advisers and his nobles like no other monarch.

And the problem is that he thought he was always right.

The other problem is that Henry desperately wanted a son. Henry realized his family the Tudors were a bit upstart, so he dreamed of his Tudor sons ruling England for a thousand years.

Henry, who had married his dead brother's wife, the Spanish princess Catherine of Aragon, was delighted when she gave birth to a son in 1511. But the baby died. Catherine gave birth to five more children. All but a girl, Mary, died.

Now girls just didn't count for Henry. No woman had ever ruled England. Women were meant to breed babies and obey their husbands, not be rulers of great kingdoms.

Henry began to grow desperate as no heir appeared and his wife started to age. In 1527 she was forty-two. His thoughts and his fancies flew to other women. Henry had always been a bit of lecher. One story tells how he saw a man called William Webbe out riding with his pretty mistress. The king took a fancy to the lady, pulled her onto his horse and took her off to his castle, to have his pleasure. The man's complaints were, as you can imagine, useless. Not to mention the lady's.

Conveniently he also began to believe that he had offended God. He found a passage in the Bible that declared that it was a sin to marry your brother's wife, and the sinner would be punished by having no children. (I know Henry and Catherine had Mary but GIRLS DIDN'T COUNT.)

Into this scene walked an enchanting creature who would change England from a Catholic to a Protestant country.

She was a rare and feisty girl, who had been living in the French king's court. Anne Boleyn, despite her long, dark hair and flashing eyes, was no conventional beauty. But she had something more powerful: keen wits and the ability to draw men to her like love-struck magnets.

Anne wasn't foolish enough to fall into Henry's arms like countless other girls (including her own sister Mary), who were then cast off. She wanted something more, to be queen.

While Henry pursued her, Anne flirted and charmed but refused to give in. He showered her with diamonds, pearls, rubies and wealth and wrote impassioned letters. 'I am struck,' he moaned to her, 'by the dart of love.' To Anne haughty Henry was almost humble, he signed himself 'your loyal servant and friend'.

But still Anne held out – for a crown.

Henry had to have her. So with the aid of his right-hand man Cardinal Wolsey, he thought up the scheme to have his marriage annulled (i.e. declared to be a sham). This meant his daughter Princess Mary was now illegitimate and no longer heir to the throne.

At the Catholic Church's headquarters in Rome, the Pope was none too pleased about Henry's plans. The powerful Spanish Emperor Charles V, who was Catherine's cousin, was outraged. Because Rome wouldn't agree to Henry's divorce, the Catholic Cardinal Wolsey was arrested for treason but unfortunately for Henry he died before he got the chance to chop his head off. However, Henry did have some consolation. He swiped Wolsey's very nice house – Hampton Court – which he had always admired.

Finally Henry found a new sidekick, Thomas Cromwell, who arranged 'Henry's little matter'. Cromwell arranged things by breaking England's thousand-year link with Rome. Between 1532 and 1534 the king became the supreme head of the Church of England, his marriage was declared void and his daughter Mary made illegitimate and no longer heir to the throne. Now he was pope as well as king in his own country. His pudgy frame bestrode the throne like no other English king!

Kicking out the Catholics was called the Reformation. Thomas Cromwell was always more keen on this than Henry (who remained a good Catholic boy at heart – perhaps he was scared of going to hell!) Monasteries were gutted and pillaged, their beautiful paintings stolen, their ornaments melted for gold and silver. Even for people who thought the Catholic church had grown too fat off the peasants' sweat and selling heavenly pardons, this was a bit rich.

In 1535 over 15,000 monks and nuns were kicked out of their monasteries and their land sold off. Guess who pocketed the money from the sale? Yep, you've got it. Henry.

Meanwhile Henry's confused people cowered in their hovels. For the first time people could be punished with death for just saying things. It became a crime to insult the new queen or to cast doubt on the new succession, i.e. who would be the next king. His minister, the famous scholar Thomas More, had his head cut off, as did another Cardinal, John Fisher, for refusing to go along with the new ways.

Now Henry was free to marry Anne, which he did, in 1533. Soon after Anne was made queen. But for Henry Anne wasn't the love to end all loves. The sort of love worth turning a kingdom upside down for.

Nope, she was the start of a marrying spree. Henry became a serial marrier, and a serial killer for that matter.

How Many Dead Wives Is That?
Henry VIII's Six Wives

1. CATHERINE OF ARAGON. Katherine was doomed when she failed to produce a male kiddywink. Anyway after twenty years of marriage, she was too pious, middle aged, plain and plain boring. DIVORCED 1533.

2. ANNE BOLEYN. Clever, headstrong Anne adored being queen. She was also was very into the new religion and advanced the Protestants by any means she could. But when

she failed to have a boy she was also doomed. (She had a girl, Elizabeth, in 1533, but how many times do I have to tell you, GIRLS DIDN'T COUNT.)

The king was getting tired of his great love, she began to nag him about his affairs with other women. She was losing her looks, the imperial ambassador now referred to her as that 'thin old woman'. Besides she stood in the way of getting chummy again with the Emperor Charles V, an alliance that was important for England. When she miscarried a dead child the king strode into her apartment and eyed her coldly: 'I see that God will not give me male children,' he said. 'When you are up I will come and speak to you.'

So Thomas Cromwell cooked up a plot against Anne. It helped his case that Anne had a big mole on her neck and a tiny sixth finger on one hand. She was accused of witchcraft and affairs with, it seemed, almost everyone (including the court musician and her brother George). Moments of flirtation were evilly twisted to make her seem guilty. Five of her supposed lovers were executed. Anne herself always swore she was innocent. She met death bravely, almost gaily, telling her jailer that she heard the sword was very sharp and 'I have a very little neck'. BEHEADED 1536.

3. JANE SEYMOUR. Nice Jane was the opposite of Anne. She kowtowed to the king in everything, she was demure and pretty. While Anne was clever and (gasp) had opinions, Jane could just about sign her name. When Anne was executed the King reined in his horse to listen contentedly to the firing of the guns. He married Jane a few days later. She was his favourite wife (later buried with him) because she gave him a son, Prince Edward, in 1537. But she died a few days later from fever. DIED 1537.

THE ONE THAT GOT AWAY

CHRISTINA OF DENMARK. Henry fell in love with the beautiful Christina of Denmark, who had been left a widow at the age of sixteen. He played her love songs deep into the night. But clever Christina, bearing in mind Henry's increasing girth and reputation, was having none of it. If I had two heads, Christina was reported to say, I would put one of them at his majesty's disposal.

4. ANNE OF CLEVES. Christina wouldn't have him and Henry had to have a new bride. The one he got by post was a German Protestant princess, whom he was told was more beautiful than Christina of Denmark. He fancied himself in love with this German chick after seeing a flattering portrait of her. But when he saw her for real he was flabbergasted by her ugliness and called her 'The Flanders

Mare'. Henry complained her body was 'loathsome' and that her smell was 'rank'. Thomas Cromwell, who had arranged the marriage which he thought would secure England new Protestant friends, bore the brunt of Henry's rage and now got his head chopped off. Unfortunately Henry couldn't give Anne of Cleves the chop because she was a princess. But he got rid of her in six months. DIVORCED 1540.

5. CATHERINE HOWARD. Now Henry's roving eye settled on a pretty, fun-loving young noblewoman. She was only twenty and Henry was nearly fifty. Though he was so fat he had to be carried around in a special chair – someone said he had enough body for a king and a half – Henry fancied Catherine was as besotted with him as he was with her. But she found him repulsive and sought comfort in the arms of a nobleman called Thomas Culpepper. When he found out Henry fell into a furious, self-pitying rage and had her executed . She died bravely, saying, 'I die a queen but I had rather died the simple wife of Tom Culpepper.' BEHEADED 1542.

6. CATHERINE PARR: Can't have been too happy when wheezing, gouty Henry asked her to be his wife, but she took the job on. Catherine Parr was a sweet-natured widow. More of a nurse to Henry than a lover, she used to let him sit with his ulcerous leg on her knees while they discussed religious problems. She was also kind to Henry's children and looked after young Princess Elizabeth till her own death in 1548. She must have thanked her lucky stars when Henry finally kicked the bucket in 1547. SURVIVED.

If you have a problem remembering Henry's six wives in order this ditty will help. DIVORCED, BEHEADED, DIED, DIVORCED, BEHEADED, SURVIVED!

CORPSE COUNT: Henry, as we know, was a serial killer as well as a serial marrier. He axed more of his courtiers, priests and lords than any other king. Not to mention peasants as well. One historian claimed he executed 70,000 people. This is a bit over the top. But he was pretty bloody all right!

TORTURE TALLY: Many of Henry's victim's only confessed after the cruellest tortures.

47

Twisted Tortures

Those happy, friendly Tudors loved a spot of torture. See if you can match some of their popular tortures against their descriptions.

A. The bootes

B. The thumbscrews

C. The bilboes

D. The piliwinks

E. The brakes

F. Tormento de toca

G. Peine forte et dure

H. The iron collar

I. The scavenger's daughter

A. Bands are screwed around the thumbs

B. Metal boots are tightened around the feet till they break the bones

C. A horrible device (worse than any dentist) for breaking prisoners' teeth (used on those accused of affairs with Catherine Howard)

D. A metal device to squeeze the ankles

E. A metal band to squeeze the fingers

F. An iron collar is tightened around the throat until the prisoner stops breathing

G. Water is poured drop by drop on your body. This drives people nuts

H. Weights are heaped on the prisoner till he is pressed to death

I. A set of irons which squeeze the body into a ball, breaking limbs and bones

CHAPTER FIVE

Bloody Mary

Queen Mary I reigned from 1553 to 1558. She got her nickname Bloody Mary because:

slurp slurp

A) She was addicted to tomato juice and vodka cocktails.

B) She was very bloody-minded and did whatever she wanted.

C) She wouldn't listen to her dad Henry VIII's pleading to go vegetarian – she insisted on stuffing herself with the bloodiest steaks going.

D) She was a Catholic fanatic and during her brief reign persecuted thousands of Protestants, 300 of whom were burnt at the stake.

ANSWER D: Bloody Mary has no problem making it onto our killer queens' hit list. She was the cause of so many deaths that her loving subjects nicknamed her Bloody Mary. For 200 years after her decease, her death was celebrated as a national holiday.

Strange to think then that as a young girl growing up Mary was a popular favourite. A tiny girl with hazel eyes and red hair she was warm-hearted, affectionate and generous. Unlike her younger sister Elizabeth, she was very sociable and loved a bit of a laugh. She was also good at her studies, Latin and music in particular.

So what happened? How did the nice, kind kid turn into the killer queen?

A lot of the nastiness that surfaced in her character later can be blamed on that old chestnut – An Unhappy Childhood.

As we already know, her dad Henry VIII was a right royal rogue. He didn't just divorce Mary's mum Katherine of Aragon, he also had a nasty habit of chopping off her stepmothers' heads.

Imagine the effect on Mary as she saw yet another stepmother taking her real mother's place. Imagine her horror as she saw yet another head rolling off the executioner's axe.

The ever-present shadow of the axe can't have made Mary feel safe and loved, can it? She had reason to fear. Anne Boleyn, Henry's second wife, was jealous of the fondness that the king harboured for his daughter. She boasted that she would make Mary: 'a maid of honour in her royal household, that she may perhaps give her too much dinner (i.e. poison her) or marry her to some varlet (rogue).'

Little wonder that when she got to the throne seventeen years later she had her revenge. At first she didn't treat her enemies too unkindly. At least by Tudor standards. She spared many of the 'traitor' lords who had tried to snatch her throne and give it to a sixteen-year-old dupe called Lady Jane Grey.

But soon Mary began to use up her popularity.

Her appeal really dropped when in July 1554 Mary married a foreign Catholic, Philip II of Spain. Spaniards were among the most hated foreigners. Many people were convinced that as a Mere Woman couldn't be a proper monarch anyway – (queens didn't count – and Mary was really the first ruling queen of England) – and that Philip would end up ruling England as king.

Mary's Phantom Child

'I have never known what it is to be happy,' Mary once wrote. Though she adored him, her husband Philip, who was eleven years younger, was bored with his religious wife. He deserted her for a life of parties and affairs with noble ladies in Europe. Imagine then Mary's joy when she became pregnant, aged thirty-nine (positively ancient to have a child in those times).

Her belly swelled and a beautiful crib, inlaid with verses celebrating the divine baby was made ready. Wet-nurses were hired, silks, satins and laces bought for the royal sproglet. Late April 1555 was the date set for the birth.

Mary and all the nobles gathered round her waited. And waited. And waited. May turned to June and still no baby appeared. The government and court was at a standstill – when would the Bloody Baby appear?

Gradually the rumours started. That Mary had given birth to a 'mole or lump of flesh'. That she intended to smuggle in a stolen child and pass it off as hers. Others said quite confidently that Mary had never been pregnant. Her belly had started to flatten, she didn't look or act pregnant. She was a foolish old maid, the gossips said, who was just kidding herself.

But Mary so wanted the child she didn't believe it. By July, two months overdue, a healthy baby would now be a miracle. Her prayer books from the time still survive. Tears have fallen on every page; most often on a prayer for the safe delivery of a pregnant woman.

The swelling in Mary's tummy was a tumour that perhaps later played a part in her early death.

The form Mary's revenge on her dad and childhood took was a Catholic fixation. All that really mattered to Queen Mary was that England revert to the true faith and become Catholic again. On this subject she became an obsessive; rebels and traitors, plotters of all sorts went free. But humble Protestants were persecuted.

The problem was that many Englishmen had decided they quite liked being Protestants. This was partly because many people hated foreigners. And the Pope was a foreigner, wasn't he? Other people resented the vast hoards of gold the Catholic Church had built up. They thought it was time it got a kick up the backside and a simpler faith take its place.

After outlawing the Protestant faith Mary really got down to business.

Most of the business was conducted with a load of

faggots, some kindling and a box of matches. Mary decided the way to persuade her subjects that Catholicism was the Word of God was to burn anyone who disagreed with her.

The first to roast was John Rogers, a leading Protestant preacher, who went to the stake at Smithfield, East London, in 1555. He went to his death promising to pray for his executioner and seemed to 'wash his hands in the flames'.

Later the Protestant bishops John Hooper, Hugh Latimer and Nicholas Ridley joined him at the stake.

The Terrible Torturing of John Hooper

Hooper was treated particularly cruelly. He was kept in the Fleet Prison in London, for two years, thrown in with criminals. He told how he was confined in a small dungeon with only a 'little pad of straw' with ticks in it to sleep on. On one side of the room ran the 'sink and filth' of the prison. On the other side the sewer. The stench made him sick. Hooper lay for days in his own poo calling for help but the guards chained his door. Finally, he prepared to die of disease.

But Mary had other plans. On a cold morning in February, after he refused to give up his Protestant faith, Hooper was brought out to be burned. But the logs were green and the fire refused to take. His feet, then his body were singed, as more logs were brought. 'For God's love, good people,' he cried out, 'bring me more fire'.

Two bags of gunpowder were tied to his legs, they were meant to explode and spare him the pain of being roasted slowly. But they failed to work and Hooper burnt for three quarters of an hour. Onlookers noted how his lips moved, praying as the flames licked his body: 'When he was black in the mouth, and his tongue swollen, that he could not speak, yet his lips went on till they were shrunk to the gums.'

To a personal enemy, Archbishop Cranmer, who had advised her dad on his divorce from her mum, Mary was even more vindictive. Cranmer had renounced his faith and claimed to be Catholic really, honest miss. He even wrote a confession of his sins. But Mary decided he was only shamming. So he was sent to burn too.

Once he knew that he had to burn Cranmer changed his mind. He said he had only pretended to renounce Catholicism so he could help people. He held his right hand out into the flames and said it must be the 'first to suffer' punishment, as it had sinned in signing his confessions.

These horrible deaths weren't just reserved for the swells. Ordinary people, labourers and peasants, bricklayers and brewers, tailors and their wives were also singled out... In fact the Protestant nobs got off pretty lightly – there were only a few of them to be burnt apart from the clergymen.

Some of the victims were just confused. Picking your religion under the Tudors was a bit of lottery – Pope rules on Monday, Pope sucks on Tuesday, Pope rules on Wednesday etc. Possibly they just got their days muddled up.

One young woman who was burnt didn't know what she was being burnt for. Another girl, a ropemaker's daughter, was blind. She couldn't even see the bishop who had sentenced her to burn. There were tales of pregnant women cast into the flames. Even the children of Protestants were sent to the stake.

Bloody Bonner

Mary couldn't have picked a fouler man to oversee the burnings in London. The fat, greedy Bishop of London Edmund Bonner was loathed. Children sang out 'Bloody Bonner' as he passed by. Their parents called him a 'beastly belly-god and damnable dung-hill'.

Bonner took an unwholesome interest in his prisoners and was said to love nothing more than a spot of torture. He liked to flog prisoners. He tortured a blind man and delighted in holding another man's hand over a candle flame until the skin cracked open.

These burnings put Londoners – most of them took place in London – right off Bloody Mary. One Protestant woman wrote to Bloody Bonner saying he had lost the hearts of twenty thousand people who had been die-hard Catholics.

Mary knew this. She knew that her burnings weren't working to make England 'pure' again. In fact as Mary sickened and died in November 1558 she may have reflected that her bloody burnings probably did more for the Protestants she so hated than all her father's rage and blustering.

CHAPTER SIX

Lethal Liz

The Tudors weren't exactly your average happy family. When Elizabeth Tudor heard that her big sister Bloody Mary had copped it, she knelt joyfully down under a huge oak tree.

'This is the Lord's doing,' she exclaimed ecstatically, 'and it is marvellous in our eyes.'

From these loving words you can see Brainy Bessie, then twenty-five, had already figured out two essentials of good royal manners:

1. Not to let family feeling get in the way of the throne. Her sister's death made her Queen Elizabeth I. Mary was equally unsisterly to Elizabeth, she had locked her up in the Tower for a while. This principle also helped her when deciding to execute her cousin Mary, Queen of Scots.

2. Never refer to yourself as just a mere person – when you can be 'our', 'we' or the whole country!

Though you wouldn't necessarily want her as a sister or cousin, Elizabeth was an amazing person. She was a born queen. During her reign, arts, the sciences and England's trade flourished. We also started taking bits of other people's countries when we fancied them. Sir Walter Raleigh wanted a bit of America, for example. He took a piece, called it Virginia (after the 'Virgin Queen') and it became the first English colony.

Brilliant Bess was also a very clever propagandist. In fact you could say she was the first modern monarch. She lavished huge amounts on a grand coronation and made sure she was very charming and gracious to ordinary people – she was constantly telling 'her people' how much she loved them and how great they were. (A good idea if you want to hang on to your crown.)

People thought it amazing she was such a powerful ruler because she was a mere, silly woman. One clergyman wrote that God must be angry with Englishmen to give the kingdom to a woman. After all, women were meant to be bossed about by their hubbies. Even Queen Bess's closest advisers, like her right-hand man, Sir William Cecil, found it hard sometimes to take her seriously. Cecil hid papers and things he thought were too 'complicated' for a woman.

In fact some of her subjects found it hard to believe in her existence at all. 'Oh Lord,' one astonished housewife exclaimed when she saw Elizabeth for the first time in a London street, 'Oh Lord! The queen is a woman.'

But Elizabeth took no notice. This may be why she never married. The men of the time were not only very unwashed and smelly, once they'd got the ring on her finger she would have been right under their thumb. There was also a serious risk of dying in childbirth.

'I am already bound unto a husband which is the kingdom of England,' she would declare, pulling her coronation ring from her finger. She kept people guessing about her marriage plans. Robert Dudley, Earl of Leicester, and the Duc D'Anjou were mentioned. But at heart Elizabeth relished the power that being the Virgin Queen gave her.

Elizabeth was fantastically clever. She could read Latin and Greek and speak French, Spanish and Italian and even Welsh. She was sometimes even quite nice (she was kind to her favourites). But she was still Henry's VIII's daughter. This meant she was capable of foulness and bloodiness in the Tudor House style. Though she never meant it as personally as did Mary, Edward and Henry.

TRUE OR FALSE: STRANGE FACTS ABOUT BESS THE BEAUT

See if you can spot which of the following weird facts are lies.

1. When thousands were dying from the plague in London Elizabeth escaped to Windsor. There she gave orders that anyone coming near her from infected areas would be hanged. Her staff set up gallows in the market place to show they meant business.

2. When she was on one of her royal tours Elizabeth had to move house every few days because she could not bear the poo and the dirt that her enormous household created.

3. She personally had a man called John Stubbs' hand cut off when he published a pamphlet objecting to her proposed marriage to a Frenchman. While his right hand was being chopped off with a cleaver Stubbs raised his hat with his left hand and cried 'God Save the Queen', before passing out.

4. She wore cherries and bits of dried sheeps' brains as earrings.

5. Elizabeth was thought to be one of the cleanest women in England because she had one of the first flush toilets ever in one of her palaces. Also she took baths – most Tudors never bathed.

6. 'My Lord, I had forgot the fart,' Elizabeth told the Earl of Oxford, who was so embarrassed at letting off in the royal presence he went into exile for seven years.

7. Elizabeth was hugely jealous of anyone who got married. She had one of her staff, Thomas Keys, who secretly married one of her ladies in waiting, Mary Grey (sister of Jane Grey, the uncrowned queen), thrown in the Fleet Prison for three years. His wife never saw him again. Nastily, Bess refused Mary permission to wear mourning when her hubby died.

8. The Pope issued a proclamation saying that anyone who killed Queen Bess would be a hero.

9. To make her complexion fashionably whiter than white, Elizabeth poisoned herself with an ointment containing white lead and vinegar. Other treats she smeared on her face included ground hogs' jawbones and asses' milk.

ANSWER: Only 4 is a lie. She did wear cherries as earrings – but never dried sheeps' brains.

Elizabeth was monstrously vain and was the biggest flirt in England – though she had no intention of going any further than flirting! She expected all her courtiers to do business with her as if they were madly, passionately in love with her.

'Would God I were with you for but one hour,' Sir Christopher Hatton, her banker, wrote to her. 'Bear with me, my most dear sweet Lady. Passion overcometh me. I can write no more. Love me, for I love you.'

If that was a letter from her banker you could imagine how Elizabeth expected her suitors to carry on. In fact in her younger days, with her red-gold hair and air of majesty, many of her courtiers did fall under her spell. But as she got older, even with her wrinkly, white-painted face, red wig and black, rotten teeth, she still expected the handsome men around her to tell her how lovely she was – how they were dying from passion for her.

'She kept the front of her dress open and you could see the whole of her bosom,' the French ambassador André Hurault wrote about the ageing Elizabeth. 'Often she would open the front of her dress as if she was too hot. She wore a reddish coloured wig ... On either side of her ears hung two curls of hair almost down to her shoulders ... Her bosom is rather wrinkled ... her face is long and thin, and her teeth are very yellow and irregular ... Many of them are missing so you cannot understand her easily when she speaks.'

Plots against Elizabeth by Catholics and desperadoes of all kinds were two-a-penny. They were often backed by foreign Catholic powers. The Spanish under her elder sister's widower King Philip were always busy scheming against her.

Scarcely had she plonked herself on the throne than a magical plot was uncovered to kill her using wax images stabbed through the heart. No wonder she got a bit paranoid. Even her own doctor, a Portuguese Jew called Ruy Lopez, was (unfairly) suspected of trying to poison her. Lopez was tortured and executed.

The Trouble with Mary

The focus of plots against Elizabeth was her beautiful Catholic cousin Mary, Queen of Scots. The queen would never be safe 'so long as that devilish woman lives', her powerful spymaster Francis Walsingham wrote. Mary was a real nuisance. Elizabeth was constantly having to execute her supporters. Both the Duke of Norfolk and Sir Francis

Throckmorton, who had separately plotted for a Spanish invasion to place Mary on the throne, were executed.

Creepy Walsingham's fingerprints were all over the most ingenious plot against Elizabeth. In 1586 Anthony Babbington, a rich Catholic nobleman, conceived a plot to make Mary queen. To do this he had to write to Mary, whom Elizabeth had locked up in a castle. Babbington found a clever way to smuggle coded letters, sealed in a waterproof pouch and then sent in kegs of beer to Mary. But he didn't know that Walsingham had arranged the secret beer post and had cracked the code.

In July 1586 Mary was silly enough to reply to Babbington. Her words had tightened the noose around her neck. Mary was arrested for treason and all fourteen of the Babbington plotters, who included a Catholic priest called John Ballard, were rounded up and brought to the Tower. They were mostly wild, romantic young men.

Ballard was the first to die; he was hanged for a bit (just to get him in the mood) and then brought down alive from the gallows. While Babbington looked on, Ballard's body was hacked to bits and his bowels were removed. This was just the start. There were to be two days of bloody executions at the Tower.

Meanwhile Mary, Queen of Scots was being held prisoner at Fotheringay Castle in Nottingham while Elizabeth hesitated over what to do with her. While she was prepared to hang, draw and quarter your average yokel traitor – killing a queen and a cousin, that was serious!

Finally after a year of hesitation on 1 February 1587 Elizabeth signed Mary's death warrant. It was swiftly put into action. Mary, queenly in a gown of black velvet and satin, lay like a calm statue on the block. The executioner botched the job and had to use the axe like a hacksaw.

The large audience watched horrified as the lips on Mary's severed head appeared to continue to pray as the executioner lifted it up by the hair. Then horror! The mass of red curls turned out to be a wig. Mary's head, with its short grey hairs, fell on the floor and rolled along like a football.

As Mary's bloody petticoat was removed a strange, wild howling sounded from within, making the audience shiver with terror. Was it a supernatural curse? It turned out to be her beloved pet terrier, which refused to be detached from Mary's body.

The terrier rejected all food and died. The little lapdog was only one of Mary's many mourners. But Elizabeth was

safer now and the twilight of her
reign was relatively free
from plots.

OK. The Spanish were
a bit peeved about
Mary's execution and
they did try to invade the
country with a huge Armada
of ships in 1588 – but the queen soon put a stop to that.

Oh, and then there was a rebellion by Elizabeth's
handsome and uppity young favourite, the Earl of Essex.
And, yes, he had to be executed too!

At the end of her days the goddess mask began to slip
from Elizabeth's wrinkled face. Tired and perhaps a little
heartsick at all the killing, she was a pale shadow of her
former regal self. But she was still the queen. When her
chief adviser told her to she 'must' go to bed for her health
she was outraged. 'Little man, little man,' she flashed back,
'the word must is not to be used to princes.'

For four days Elizabeth sat alone on a pile of cushions in
her chamber, refusing food and drink, starving to death. On
the third day she put her finger in her mouth and rarely
took it out afterwards.

At last she grew so weak that her doctors were able to carry her to bed. There she turned her face to the wall and died. She was sixty-nine and had ruled for nearly half a century.

CORPSE COUNT: The graveyards filled up with Elizabeth's victims. Towards the end of Elizabeth's reign the German Paul Hentzner counted 300 heads stuck on London Bridge of those executed for treason. But Elizabeth *was* the most plotted against monarch in English history.

TORTURE TALLY: Elizabeth didn't really like blood and when she heard how the first Babbington conspirators to die were tortured, she had the rest simply hanged. But Elizabeth's reign was still the worst time ever for terrible tortures in the Tower.

CHAPTER SEVEN

James the Paranoid

James I succeeded Elizabeth to the English throne. He was the son of Mary, Queen of Scots and was the Scottish King James VI, before he got his fingers on the English crown. When he was crowned king at Westminster thousands of his new English citizens flocked to see him. They lined the roads, cheering his royal party to the skies as it rode triumphantly into London. But it didn't take his citizens long to change their minds. To get things going a couple of unattractive traits put them off their new king.

1) James just didn't seem very kingly. Admittedly, this wasn't his fault. Here is what one unimpressed courtier, Anthony Weldon, had to say about him:

His beard was very thin, his tongue too large for his mouth, which ... made him drink very uncomely, as if eating his drink, which came out of his cup each side of his mouth ... his walk was ever circular, his fingers ever in that walk fiddling with that codpiece* ... he would never change his clothes until worn to very rags.

(*A codpiece is a metal structure worn over the private parts)

2) After ruling a relatively poor country (Scotland) James couldn't believe how rich he was as King of England. As King of the Scots he had had to get by on £50,000 (a wealthy landowner would have about £3,000 a year). He called his first years in London 'Christmas time'. He was gross and greedy for all good things – food, wine, silks and satins. To his people's dismay he began to spend, spend, spend. In 1604 he splashed out £47,000 on jewels. And the money eventually came out of the people's pockets through more taxes.

When they looked at James his subjects saw a gross man, who lived it up like no one's business. OK, monarchs were practically gods on earth. But this was not the way to endear him to his people.

More grub, please

What was an ante-supper at King James's court?

1. The nobles would all do yoga to prepare themselves for much feasting

2. They would perform knightly acts with lances and horses to show off

3. A lavish banquet before the real supper – which would be thrown away untasted to be replaced by another even more lavish banquet

Answer:

3. The amount of wasted food at James's court was phenomenal. On 12 December 1621 one of James's favourites gave him a modest little supper party. To prepare for this one hundred cooks spent twelve days preparing 1600 dishes. One waiter at the dinner smuggled out a pie from the ante-supper that had been thrown away, without a bite being taken out of it. The pie was made of 'ambergris, magisterial of pearl, musk etc'. Unfortunately it was so rich that it gave the waiter's family food poisoning. The waiter's family were probably very hungry. Ordinary Londoners had a horrible diet. They scraped by on a diet of yucky dark bread, oats, acorns, beer (because the water was unfit to drink) and if they were lucky cheese and milk. Meat was a real luxury.

..Why is Daddy in bits on the floor?...
........James's early life..........

In James's defence he did have a horrid time as he was growing up. His family life probably made him long to be an orphan. (He didn't have long to wait.) While little Jamie was just a baby in his mother's womb he had his first exposure to murder. In 1566 his mother, Mary, Queen of Scots, watched while her boyfriend David Riccio was knifed to death.

Things didn't get better. When James was a baby of eight months his dad, Lord Darnley, was strangled and blown up outside Edinburgh. Confusingly his mum later married the man accused of his dad's murder – James, Earl of Bothwell. This marriage was very unpopular and Mary had to give up the throne to her baby son and flee to England – where she was promptly locked up by Elizabeth.

Now James had a series of guardians looking after him.
(The most jinxed job in Scotland.)
Moray, his uncle, was assassinated in 1570.
The Earl of Lennox, his grandad, was killed in 1571.
The Earl of Mar died, unbelievably, of natural causes in 1572.
The Earl of Morton was executed in 1581 for the murder of James's dad.
And, to cap it all, his mother was beheaded.

Little wonder then that James was a tad paranoid. And he had reason to be. The plots around him and against his life continued.

The weirdest plot involved witches and wizards – and gave James a lifelong fascination with black magic. He even published a book about witches called *Daemonologie*.

In 1591 James was on his way overseas to see his future bride, Princess Anne of Denmark. Suddenly a great storm blew up and the royal party was nearly drowned.

The storm was blamed on witchcraft. A coven of witches, led by a schoolmaster-wizard called John Fian, had caused the storm. To do this they had thrown a dead cat and parts of a dead body into the sea and chanted spells. The witches were caught and horribly tortured – before being put to death.

James was initially a bit dubious about the confessions of the witches. But he was convinced when one of them, Agnes Sampson, told him the very words he had exchanged with Princess Anne in the privacy of their bedroom on their wedding night. He 'acknowledged her words to bee most true and therefore gave the more credit' to their stories.

Ghoulishly James took a close personal interest in the

witch trial. He watched 'with great delight' while Fian was tortured. All Fian's fingernails were pulled out with pincers and needles inserted under what was left of them. His feet were crushed horribly in an iron device called 'the bootes' that got smaller and smaller. Finally Fian was strangled and burned at the stake!

James had a reputation as a bit of a clever-clogs. (Perhaps because he wrote books. Some kings weren't too hot on joined-up letters.) But when he became king of England he wanted to concentrate on eating, drinking, hunting and showering his handsome, lordly 'favourites' with money and jewels. The real governing of England he left to his right-hand man Lord Cecil, who was very overworked.

These pretty young lords became King James's obsession and he virtually bankrupted the nation's coffers treating them to all sorts of luxuries. The very good-looking James Hay, whom the king made Earl of Carlisle, pocketed £400,000 of the Crown's dosh. Hay's motto was 'Spend and the Lord will send'. Mostly Hay spent England's money on gambling, whoring, fab clothes and (of course) eating and drinking.

Another favourite, George 'Steenie' Villiers, was made Duke of Buckingham. James had taken a shine to his 'lovely complexion' after watching him 'leap and exercise' his body with other young men after supper. He took to wearing Steenie's picture hanging from a blue ribbon over his heart.

One courtier commented: 'The setting up of these golden calves (young blokes) cost England more than Queen Elizabeth had spent in all her wars.'

But James couldn't just concentrate on witches, lovely young men, hunting, eating and drinking. There were more plots against his Scottish royal person.

The most famous was the Gunpowder Plot.

The background to this famous plot was religion. Catholics in England, who after Protestant Elizabeth's death, hoped James would be much, much nicer to them. After all his missus Anne was a Catholic. But though he didn't seem to have strong, personal feelings on the subject, James wasn't exactly soft on Catholics. By 1605 he had ordered all

Catholic priests out of the country. Lots of Catholics started to get very cheesed off.

In 1605 a hot-headed Catholic nobleman, Robert Catesby, dreamed up an audacious plot to blow up Parliament and the king. The plotters were caught after one of them wrote to a Catholic lord warning him to stay clear of Parliament. The lord went straight to the government.

James took a close personal interest in the plotters' punishment. He wrote: 'The gentler tortures are to be first used on Guy Fawkes and so on step by step to the most severe and so God speed your good work.'

Here is what Guy Fawkes (yep, the one we make out of straw and sling on top of a bonfire every year) might have had to say about his part in the plot ...

THE TOWER OF LONDON VISITORS BOOK

6 November 1605

The dreary hours of the night are the only time I have to be alone with my conscience. I declare loudly, my conscience is clear.

Pretending to be one John Johnson I did, along with others who are true to the Catholic faith, plot to blow up the King and Parliament. The gunpowder was all stacked in bags in the cellars under Parliament, the fuses, the kindling, the matches were ready. We were hours from the big bang — when the King's soldiers burst in.

I tell you all this proudly. Many would have died, true. But the greater good was a noble one. God and the Pope looked on it with favour.

But for ill luck we would have blown those Protestant tyrants to the sky and Englishmen would once more be free. But I mustn't muse on the past. I must conserve my strength not to betray my faith.

Today I spent many hours in Little Ease. This dungeon is so tiny it is not possible to either lie down or stand up in it. One must crouch naked and shivering, for hours, like a wild beast.

This I think was to soften me up. Conceive my surprise when I was taken to the Royal bedchamber itself. James — who is as ugly as they say — lolled on his puffed and primped cushions. He looked greasy and dirty. Idling around him were handsome young men dressed in silks, satins and jewels.

The king himself questioned me. Again and again he asked me who my accomplices were. Who paid me? How had I dared to try and blow up a king? But I told him nothing. He seems to me more like a common jackanapes than a king. God willing my fellows in this plot will escape.

Later I was taken back to the Tower. To the torture dungeons. There I was hung from the ceiling in manacles — while the king's henchman, Lord Cecil, and others taunted me with my crimes. But I am a soldier. I will not break or betray my friends.

So I was placed on the rack. Slowly, while pain racked every bone and sinew in my body, I was stretched apart. Aching, aching pain. My limbs were on fire; my legs parting from my stomach, my head from my neck. I prayed to God to let me die. But the torture went on and on.

I could stand it no longer and confessed all. To make it stop, please god.

The other plotters were equally well treated by James's men. Eight of them were dragged in the dirt on wicker mats behind horses, as their wives and children watched in the howling mob. One little boy called out 'Tata, Tata' to his daddy.

Then they were hanged, cut down while still alive and their bowels taken out. After this their private parts and hearts were cut off and bits of their bodies were displayed, like Christmas decorations, around London.

Still, these plotters did try and blow him to smithereens.

But James really had very little reason to lock up Sir Walter Raleigh, the famous Elizabethan explorer, writer, scientist, all-round genius and introducer to tobacco to England. (Apart from a trumped-up treason charge based on jealousy, perhaps.)

Raleigh was the most popular prisoner the Tower would ever hold and people flocked to see him taking his daily stroll on the battlements. Nobles and foreign scholars, the queen and James's popular oldest son Prince Henry came to see Raleigh. Prince Henry said of him, 'Only my father would keep such a bird in his cage.'

Raleigh was treated relatively well – for a while he was allowed to have his wife live with him. Then Jealous James finally decided to chop off his head in 1618.

THE TOWER OF LONDON VISITORS BOOK

Sir Walter Raleigh 1 6 18

Hmm, I must just light
myself a quick, healthy pipe
to clear my lungs before I
jot down a quick word of
appreciation for the
service and facilities here.

Admittedly I have spent
rather longer in the Bloody Tower (rather a tasteless name, I think) than
I would have wished. It is thirteen years so far. But my time here has been,
if not exactly pleasant, productive enough.

Alas, I will not have time to finish my masterpiece, 'The History of the
World'. But I had my little hen-house where I brewed my potions and
conducted experiments. People have been good enough to say that my
potions have helped them recover from most unpleasant illnesses.

And I have enjoyed building my little model ships. So the time has passed
swiftly enough. The food and lodgings have been good and I have nothing
but praise for the staff here who looked after me so well. One little
whinge — was it really necessary for the warder to lock me up in the damp
basement? It gave me terrible rheumatism.

Well, thanking you all for making my stay as homely as possible. And I do hope you enjoy my execution tomorrow. I believe it is scheduled for midday but do please check the time!

Raleigh met death bravely. He asked the executioner to feel the axe to see if it was sharp enough. 'This is sharp medicine,' he said, 'but it is a physician for all diseases.' He told him to strike his head off when he raised his hands.

When the axeman asked Raleigh if he wished to be blindfolded he replied that he was not likely to fear the shadow of the axe, as he did not fear the axe itself.

Raleigh gave the signal to cut off his head. But the executioner was shaking so much he couldn't do it. 'What dost thou fear?' Raleigh asked. 'Strike, man, strike.' Trembling, the axeman muffed his blow, and had to strike again. Then he held up the head by its hair – to dead silence from the normally rowdy crowd.

In the stillness a man from the crowd called out 'We have not another such head to cut off.'

When James himself snuffed it in 1625 there was no one around to give him such a heart-felt send-off. He wasn't that popular with his people. He once said, when told the common folk wanted to see his face: 'God's wounds! I will pull down my breeches and they will also see my arse.' So no surprise that his demise was met by a notable lack of weeping in the streets.

CORPSE COUNT: The schoolmaster-wizard John Fian and his witches, Guy Fawkes and his accomplices just for starters. (OK, they did plot against him). But James did seem to like to watch torture, the more hideous the better. And then Sir Walter Raleigh. Not a good record.

TORTURE TALLY: Again James did take a bit too much of an interest in the bootes, manacles etc.

CHAPTER EIGHT

James the Useless

Like his grandfather James I, James II had a pretty bloody childhood. His dad Charles I was fantastically unpopular, for his extravagance, political stupidity and general block-headedness. While little Jamie was still a wee boy, Charles's people rose against him. Young James was horrified when his dad became the first (and so far only) English king to get his head chopped off by his subjects. Oliver Cromwell's fanatically Protestant 'Roundheads' did the gruesome deed.

James II was more ingenious than his dad and managed to escape from the Roundheads. On 21 April 1646 James slipped out of the palace where he was being held in London and met an accomplice. Dressed in women's clothes the fourteen-year-old James took a barge from London Bridge and then a ship to Holland. The bargemaster apparently suspected the young lady's virtue when she hitched her stockings up very clumsily and allowed her friend to tie her garter.

Thirty-nine years later, in 1685, James became King James II, succeeding his brother Charles II. Charlie had energetically fathered children – but not with his wife.

Right from the off James was unpopular.

For a start he was a Catholic and the English were now by and large convinced Protestants. They were scared that James might make everyone attend the Catholic mass. Worse, they thought he might start chopping the heads off Protestants.

On the surface James was all pious and moral. He stopped spending money like it had gone out of fashion – unlike his wasteful brother and father. He announced that he would not employ people who were drunkards, gamblers, swearers or adulterers.

But he hardly practised what he preached. In fact he spent huge amounts of his time leching after other women. The diary writer, Samuel Pepys, said he was the biggest 'ogler' he had ever seen. James kept a secret apartment at Whitehall for his mistresses and often smuggled women he took a fancy to up the backstairs to his rooms.

Poor James wasn't the smartest king on the block and he hadn't learnt much from his dad's mistakes. He persisted in thinking that as KING, he was a mighty ruler who didn't need to listen to anyone. Thus he made few friends, certainly not among members of Parliament, who had got a taste for making laws lately.

Scarcely had James plonked himself on the throne than he faced a rebellion from his nephew. The Duke of Monmouth was a handsome young Protestant, who was Charles II's illegitimate son, James's nephew. He landed in Lyme Regis, south-west England in June 1685 – and soon an army of 4,000 men had flocked to him.

Most were poor workers, farmers and craftsmen. They were a motley army and they were soon routed by James's 30,000 ferocious professional soldiers. Monmouth escaped and swapped clothes with a shepherd. James's men first found the swankily dressed shepherd standing at a crossroad – then Monmouth cowering in a heap of hay.

Though his nephew begged for mercy, James was determined to get his pint of blood. The axeman chopped and chopped away at Monmouth's head – but it wouldn't come off. Finally it parted from his body. Then someone realized there was no proper portrait of Monmouth.

On the principle of better late than never, the poor duke's head was sewn back onto his body, he was stuffed in a chair and an artist was told to paint him. The result can still be seen in the National Portrait Gallery – try and spot the joins where Monmouth's head is stitched back on!

James's treatment of the poor working men who joined Monmouth's rebellion was even worse. At the Bloody Assizes in Somerset a sadist called Judge Jeffreys hanged, drew and quartered three hundred men. The ground ran ankle-deep in blood. Other rebels were transported to the colonies as slaves – which was a virtual death sentence. James's ghoulish courtiers competed for their property. Jeffreys wrote to the king saying the prisoners were worth ten to fifteen pounds each and he feared unworthy people would 'run away with the booty'.

James showed what he thought of Jeffreys' vile 'campaign' by promoting him to Lord Chancellor.

The Warming Pan Baby

James's queen Mary Beatrice announced in January 1688 that she was pregnant and that the baby was a son and heir to the throne! How did she know, people wondered? The country was in uproar. The last thing most people wanted was a Catholic heir to the throne. Indeed many were hoping that James's Protestant daughter Mary, who was married to the Dutch Prince William of Orange, would take over when he pegged it.

Soon rumours of foul play bounced around. As the queen got bigger her sister-in-law thought it was a 'false belly' – else why she didn't let anyone near her stomach?

Meanwhile James was pressing ahead with his plans to make England more Catholic – much to his bishops' dismay!

In June 1688 the son, James Edward, was born. His dad fell to his knees and wept. But others said a different baby had been smuggled into the royal rooms in a warming pan (a sort of early hot-water bottle). A priest was said to have been paid for his son. James tried to put paid to the rumours by having forty-two men and women swear that they knew the young prince to be the king's son. But the rumours spread.

By now James was thoroughly unpopular. Seven politicians decided to act. They sent an invitation to the Dutch William of Orange to invade the country. The invitation basically went like this:

Dear Will,

We are fed up with James. He has 'greatly invaded' our 'religion and liberties'.

So please invade for real.

Love 'The Immortal Seven'

William obliged by sending in an army of 500 boats with 20,000 soldiers and 7,000 horses. 'I come to do you goot,' he told the crowd waiting for him at Bridport. James was outraged that his little daughter and her hubby could treat him like that – he got an army of 25,000 soldiers together and marched towards Salisbury.

But though he loved to play at war, when the crunch came James went to pieces. Blood kept gushing out of his nose and several of his major commanders deserted. Panicking, James disbanded his army and rushed back to London to chuck his royal seal* in the Thames and try and flee the country. He escaped from Whitehall Palace by using the privy (toilet) stairs. William meanwhile stopped off to look at some choice pictures by a Dutch painter on his leisurely journey to London – which was more like a coronation procession than what it was – an invasion.

(*No, not a cute royal pet but a kind of stamp that worked as a signature of his authority)

The 'Glorious Revolution' was the most bizarre revolution/invasion in our history. It had been achieved without a drop of blood. William and Mary became the new king and queen – and James II skulked away to the continent.

After the glorious revolution of 1668 in which King William and Queen Mary took over the throne, our rulers were never quite so bloody again. Was this because?

A) Our ancestors were barbarians – basically as time went on even kings and queens became more civilized and less bloody.

B) Monarchs had a better diet with more vitamins – therefore they were less prone to chopping off people's heads in a foul rage.

C) A Bill of Rights restricted the power of monarchs.

D) Parliament fined kings and queens £1,000,000 for every head they chopped off! Most monarchs were too mean to pay the fines.

E) Murder became less trendy.

ANSWER: C. Parliament brought in the Bill of Rights, which was the beginning of the modern 'constitutional monarchy' (which means the monarch has to listen to Parliament). The Bill of Rights said among other things the sovereign couldn't just ditch the laws when it suited and that Parliament could control their spending. Oh, and people (except Catholics) could worship how they chose.

We're in a small, hot basement. There is no sunlight, instead everything is lit by the sickly, yellow glow of flames. A strong smell of sulphur lingers over the scene. In one corner Lucifer is toasting muffins, dotted with eyes, on his pitchfork.

Crowded around a shabby table are a bunch of seedy men and women. They are a wrinkled and rouged group of pug-uglies and have certainly not dressed for the heat. They are absolutely sweltering in all their finery: ruffs, jewels, silks, satins and crowns.

ELIZABETH I: *(her long nose wrinkling with distaste)* I really don't see why I'm here. I always had a horror of bloodshed.

JAMES I: You certainly failed to take an interest in the details. *(He twiddles self-consciously with his crown)* I always thought watching made the whole torture thing more fun. But, my dear auntie, you were certainly very bloody.'

(Elizabeth looks sour and proud)

BLOODY MARY: 'Face it, Liz, you were absolutely loathsome. *(Getting up impatiently, sweat is running in streaks down her face, leaving track-marks in her thick face powder)* For Godsake's. Can someone turn the central heating down? It's like a furnace in here!

KING JOHN: Dear girl, God has nothing to do with this hellhole. Don't you realize, this is a furnace? We are suffering the fires of eternal damnation. Fine for you lot. But I was always a cut above!

JAMES II: Oh shut up, you soap-smelling whinger. What I want to know is, who wins? Who is the BLOODIEST monarch of us all?

HENRY VIII: Surely it's MOI. I did kill a couple of my wives after all. Or was it more? One does so forget with time. There were so many of them, you see...

WILLIAM THE CONQUEROR: Killing a few women 'ardly compares wiz ze pillaging and ze burning of 'of villages. I 'ave 'ad more people put to ze stake zan you 'ad 'ot croissants.

RICHARD III: Codswallop. I think that the most bloody crimes of all are those of one's nearest, if not dearest. Poor little things, putting their faith so in one. Heh, heh, heh ... Could someone scratch me hump for me?

So who do you think was the bloodiest monarch to have graced the city?

Other books from Watling St you'll love

CRYPTS, CAVES AND TUNNELS OF LONDON
By Ian Marchant
Peel away the layers under your feet and discover the unseen treasures of London beneath the streets.
ISBN 1-904153-04-6

GRAVE-ROBBERS, CUT-THROATS AND POISONERS OF LONDON
By Helen Smith
Dive into London's criminal past and meet some of its thieves, murderers and villains.
ISBN 1-904153-00-3

DUNGEONS, GALLOWS AND SEVERED HEADS OF LONDON
By Travis Elborough
For spine-chilling tortures and blood-curdling punishments, not to mention the most revolting dungeons and prisons you can imagine.
ISBN 1-904153-03-8

THE BLACK DEATH AND OTHER PLAGUES OF LONDON
By Natasha Narayan
Read about some of the most vile and rampant diseases ever known and how Londoners overcame them – or not!
ISBN 1-904153-01-1

GHOSTS, GHOULS AND PHANTOMS OF LONDON
By Travis Elborough
Meet some of the victims of London's bloodthirsty monarchs, murderers, plagues, fires and famines – who've chosen to stick around!
ISBN 1-904153-02-X

RATS, BATS, FROGS AND BOGS OF LONDON
By Chris McLaren
Find out where you can find some of the creepiest and crawliest inhabitants of London.
ISBN 1-904153-05-4

HIGHWAYMEN, OUTLAWS AND BANDITS OF LONDON
By Travis Elborough
Take yourself back to the days when the streets of London hummed with the hooves of highwaymen's horses and the melodic sound of 'Stand and deliver!'
ISBN 1-904153-13-5

SPIES, SECRET AGENTS AND BANDITS OF LONDON
By Natasha Narayan
Look through the spy hole at some of our greatest spies and their exploits, to how to make your own invisible ink.
ISBN 1-904153-14-3

PIRATES, SWASHBUCKLERS AND BUCCANEERS OF LONDON
By Helen Smith
Experience the pockmarked and perilous life of an average London pirate and his (or her) adventures.
ISBN 1-904153-17-8

REBELS, TRAITORS AND TURNCOATS OF LONDON
By Travis Elborough
What could you expect if you were a traitor – and you were discovered? Take your pick from some of the most hideous punishments ever invented.
ISBN 1-904153-15-1

WITCHES, WIZARDS AND WARLOCKS OF LONDON
By Natasha Narayan
Quite simply the bizarre history of London, full of superstition, magic and plain madness.
ISBN 1-904153-12-7

In case you have difficulty finding any Watling St books in your local bookshop, you can place orders directly through

BOOKPOST
Freepost
PO Box 29
Douglas
Isle of Man
IM99 1BQ

Telephone: 01624 836000

email: bookshop@enterprise.net